Princess' Pony Club

Princesses Picnic

Princess Violet

Princess Evergreen

Best Friends Princesses

Princess Fairy Steps

Princess Daydream

Princess Valentine

Clumsy Princess

Princess Bride

Princess Serenade

Princess Starlight

Sleepy Princess

Rescue Me

Caring Princess

Boating Princess